About the Saltire Society

We are:

An apolitical membership organisation open to all

*

An international supporter and patron of the arts and cultural
heritage of Scotland

*

A champion of free speech on the issues that matter to the
cultural life of every Scot

*

A promoter of the best of what we are culturally, now and
in the future

*

A catalyst to ensure new ideas are considered and the best of
them are made real.

We believe we have an important and unique role to play as
an independent advocate and celebrant of all that is good and
important about our cultural lives and achievements.
The Society has played a crucial role over the last 75 years
in recognising our cultural achievements. And while times
have changed, the need for the independent voice remains.

GW00691979

Editorial note

In the Saltire Series we have invited individuals to spark fresh thinking, ignite debate and challenge our orthodoxies, through the publication of short commissioned essays. The Editorial note from a pamphlet produced in 1942 is still a strong expression of the proposition:

> They will express the considered judgements of their own authors, to whom complete freedom has been given; and are not to be taken as representing the policy of the Saltire Society, whose objective is to promote that free and informed discussion without which no sound policy for Scotland's future can be shaped.

In this publication we have partnered the Scottish Poetry Library, our neighbours down the Canongate, in publishing poems commissioned from three of the most distinguished older poets now working in Scotland, with support from the Baring Foundation's series of 'Late Style' artist commissions. According to the Scottish Government's demographics, based on the 2013 census, projections suggest that by 2037 the population will age significantly, with the number of people aged 65 and over increasing by 59%, from 0.93 million to 1.47 million. Our thinking behind the series holds good: here are poems that spark fresh thinking and challenge the orthodoxies surrounding ageing in particular.

If you wish to comment on or discuss this pamphlet please visit: www.saltiresociety.org.uk/discuss-and-debate

SECOND WIND

From left to right: Diana Hendry, Vicki Feaver, Douglas Dunn

Photograph by Peter Adamson

SECOND WIND

New Poems

Douglas Dunn
Vicki Feaver
Diana Hendry

SALTIRE SERIES NO. 9

Published in 2015 by
The Saltire Society
9 Fountain Close
22 High Street
Edinburgh
EH1 1TF
www.saltiresociety.org.uk

in association with the
Scottish Poetry Library
5 Crichton's Close
Edinburgh
EH8 8DT
www.scottishpoetrylibrary.org.uk

Thanks to the editors of the magazines where some of these poems
have appeared: Douglas Dunn's '"Wondrous Strange"' in Ploughshares,
'Cognitive Disorders' and 'Curmudgeon' in the Scottish Review of Books;
Vicki Feaver's 'The Blue Wave' and 'Forgetfulness' in the Scottish Review of Books,
'Death and the Maiden' in The Dark Horse, 'Prayer at Seventy' in Poetry Review;
Diana Hendry's 'First Love' in The Spectator, 'Beyond' and 'Timor Mortis…' in
the Scottish Review of Books.

ISBN 978-0-85411-120-6

Designed and typeset by Gerry Cambridge
www.gerrycambridge.com

Cover image by Alasdair Gray

PRINTED BY CHARLESWORTH PRESS

Contents

DOUGLAS DUNN

Introduction: Ageing · 9
Thursday · 11
Leaving the Office · 12
The Wash · 13
'Wondrous Strange' · 15
Cognitive Disorders · 16
Older Poet to Younger Poets · 17
The Nothing-But · 19
Progress · 20
Curmudgeon · 21
Recipes and Refugees · 22
In a Volume of Dowson's · 24
The Glove Compartment · 26
Remembering Friends Who Feared Old Age
    and Dementia More than Death · 27

VICKI FEAVER

Introduction: Riding a Wave · 29
Forgetfulness · 31
The Larder · 32
Bone-House · 33
Pomegranate Juice · 35
Old Woman in a Forsythia Bush · 36
The Mower · 37
Travelling · 38
The Blue Wave · 39
The Old Fir-Tree · 40
Swimming in Old Age · 42
Dreams of Flying · 43
Clementines · 45

Second Childhood · 46
Costume Boxes · 47
Prayer at Seventy · 48
Death and the Maiden · 49
Instructions for My Funeral · 51

DIANA HENDRY

Introduction: Off / On Joy · 53
Callers · 55
The House Where I Was Born · 56
Autobiography · 57
Beyond · 58
Parting · 59
Teeth · 60
The Cut · 61
Charades with Freya (7) · 62
Meditation on an Old Bear · 63
The Widow · 64
Insomnia · 65
An Alternative Retirement · 66
My First Love · 67
Watching Telly With You · 68
Timor mortis conturbat me · 69
End Matter · 70
The Last Piano · 71
Praise Poem · 72

Douglas Dunn: Ageing

In thinking about 'ageing', I re-read some Shakespeare. Melancholy Jacques's famous if misanthropic speech in As You Like It struck me as a possible beginning, but turned out not to be. You'll remember that his 'seven ages' begins with 'the infant, muling and puking', and ends with 'second childishness and mere oblivion, / Sans teeth, sans eyes, sans taste, sans everything.' In Freudian terms, Jacques is Thanatos intruding on the court of Eros. I wouldn't do that. Then I re-read Henry IV Part 2 and Falstaff saying 'We have heard the chimes at midnight, Master Shallow.' Roger that, I thought. An evening with King Lear could have shut me up for ever, so great is its poetic power even after many years of familiarity.

Other reading helped. Books by the late Oliver Sacks, for example. His writing suggested to me that imagination, the perception of what might not be real, or present, is not far distant from hallucinations caused by neurological or substance-induced trauma—'Cognitive Disorders' and '"Wondrous Strange"' owe something to that reading but as much or more to my own imaginative experience in recent years. Also, retirement suggested itself as a subject, and its imminence is reflected in 'Thursday' (always, for some reason, the busiest day of my working week as a professor at St Andrews), while its fact appears in 'Leaving the Office', getting rid of student- and staff-generated bumph, with greatly appreciated and invaluable assistance. 'The Wash' draws from a conversation I had with a dear friend, the late Ian Hamilton, when I suggested that reputation doesn't matter, it all comes out eventually in the wash. He disagreed, and in his introduction to his Oxford Companion to Twentieth-Century Poetry he seems to have remembered this when he points out that a dead poet's work needs a critic-champion to perpetuate it. In any case, the sense of being overtaken by younger poets is probably inevitable, and it's a good idea to feel benign about it. 'Older Poet to Younger Poets' probably depends on my life as a teacher of literature, on the habits of pedagogy, although I hope it encourages independence of thought and, above all, openness to sensory experience.

Other subjects addressed here (although I don't always write 'aboutly')
include 'giving up the car' ('The Glove Compartment'), and first love 'In A
Volume of Dowson' (inevitable for a man in his seventies). Equally to be
anticipated is the fear of senility or death ('Remembering Friends …').

I am very grateful to the Scottish Poetry Library and The Baring
Foundation for commissioning these poems. It has also been a great
pleasure to work with Vicki Feaver and Diana Hendry, and with Lilias
Fraser, Amy McDonald, Robyn Marsack and Colin Waters.

*

Douglas Dunn (born 1942) lives in Fife. He has published
14 collections of poetry and edited several anthologies.
Elegies (1985), a moving series of poems on his first wife's
death, won the Whitbread Prize. He became a Professor
of English at the University of St Andrews in 1991, and holds
an OBE and the Queen's Gold Medal for Poetry.

Thursday

Gave yet another lecture. God, I'm boring.
Said all the same old things I've said before
With touches of 'however-ing' and 'therefore-ing'.
Dear God, it's true, I'm just an ancient bore.

If only I could tap my old exuberance,
High spirits that I plied in days of yore,
Then maybe I would find a kind deliverance
From the curse of being such a bloody bore.

For I'm the model of a modern academic.
I'm absolutely super at ennui.
I'm just stunning when it comes to a polemic,
And boredom's snoredom's what I guarantee.

I'm putting extra pennies in my pension.
Retirement beckons and the garden calls,
That beautiful, botanical dimension
Where boilersuited pensioners scratch their balls.

But I've a problem, and it's called 'work ethic', so
I'll slog on with the daily, dreary toil.
Heigh-ho, heigh-ho, what a lousy way to go,
To work all day then burn the midnight oil.

Leaving the Office

For Frances

Somehow it all gets done and over with—
The office emptied of its archival dross,
Papers re-read, and chucked, the years of breath
Re-breathed, moment by moment. Why feel cross
At this departure? Why feel worse than sad
For fag-ashed, faded memos, decisions taken,
Or not taken, the good, indifferent, bad,
Right ways of doing, and the mistaken?

Permit no tears, but still, allow a sigh
Closing a door on what was once my life,
My days, my work. Farewell, and so goodbye
While haar is forming over North-East Fife.
It's like *The Cruel Sea*, the ship going down—
Jack Hawkins with his duffel-coated frown.

'Confidential books over the side? Carry on.'
We should have lit a bonfire on the lawn,
Thrown on the lot. Instead, my Number One
Lugs binbags to the shredder, day by day,
As slow as patient archaeology.
Shiver me timbers! But it's not much fun.

Not pushed, but oh-so-very-gently shoved
Towards the book-loaded van and a pension,
Then shelving shadows with the books I've loved.

The Wash

Reading younger contemporaries

So much time wasted wanting to be remembered
Ends with desire to be forgotten,
As one chirrup absent from the dawn chorus,
An unclaimed seat in the theatre,
A volume missing from the library shelf.

Ambition determines you, then trips over itself;
But I was never a self-lover, or a self-hater.
Is it age that creates this feeling, to bore us,
Or twisted self-knowledge gone rotten,
Or dreams allowed to be dismembered?

I look at the Spring's predictable daffodils
Bugling yellow silences, snowdrops and crocus
Already gone, fritillaries a-bloom,
Tulips, bluebells and others still to come,
And summer's lilies, lupins, and roses.

And all the rest of them, florals and edibles,
And all the rest of botanical hocus-pocus
In seasonal wonder, marguerites, delphinium,
Periwinkles to be pressed in a slim volume,
Honeysuckle, marigolds, whatever Hortus proposes.

It all depends on the luck of the weather,
As everything else does, in a sense,
And everyone. It all comes out in the wash?
Hmn. But it could be in someone else's favour,
With the gale and the sleet in your girning face.

Better off forgotten, like scorched heather,
Your weathered and withered intelligence,

Your talent thinning like hair, maladroit tosh
Set down in a notebook as if to savour
Another stab at despair and disgrace.

It's odd how ambition stumbles, and falls,
As the young overtake you, with a pat on the back,
If you're lucky, a smile from over the shoulder.
I did that too. Or I suppose I did.
No harm intended; it's just the way it is,

The way of the world, with its doors and its walls.
Is this all because I've no Muse in my sack?
I don't feel like Sisyphus, I feel like his boulder—
Something used, or abused, for a task that's not ended,
That won't be, and certainly not with this.

So, fall off a barstool swigging your hemlock
For what we have here is perseverance's tedium.
The bowler's seven feet tall and very fast,
Their striker kicks like a camel and you're in goal,
Their scrum-half's fleet-footed as destiny.

Don't worry. Your reputation's safe with me,
Old pal of mine, shadow, my friend, old chum.
How long does a book, or sheet of paper, last?
If the answer is hundreds of years, does that console?
Go early to bed and outstare the clock.

'Wondrous Strange'

Now it can almost be heard. But not quite
Almost. Still on the far side of nearly,
It is the melody of a floating feather.

A spiderweb fingers my cheek in the dark garden;
A briar plucks at my sweater.
Wind on a windless night wafts through my hair.

Or the aroma of sandalwood soap
When that's impossible. Or of fenugreek,
Or the scent of one who is no longer here.

Or something I half-believe I've seen,
A glisk of movement on the hill's horizon,
An ominous shadow cast by nothing at all.

Then there's the taste of zero-flavour,
Not even the taste of my own mouth,
Neither sweet and delicious, or bitter or sour.

Or the taste of strawberries Romanov
(That restaurant in Bonn!) or stolen plums
Remembered on a January night when snow's falling.

Is this just dream-stuff, or is there enough
Sense in the senses for the mystical
To prove itself real as any truth?

Yes, it's 'wondrous strange'; but I must ask
My Muse to save me from contriving
A forger's touch of moonlight on the page.

Cognitive Disorders

'Butterflies rock no cradles, nor do they sing.'
Or so a mad poet writes down on his page.
'I've listened, looked; can't hear or see a thing
Other than snails on their silky pilgrimage
Over the slippery slabs of a garden path.
I've heard ants' martial marching songs,
Their tiny tambourines, trumpets, and gongs,
Too-whoos of the nocturnal polymath.
I've heard the patient moans of mushrooms growing
Where bees coax ding-dongs from a foxglove's bells,
A spider crooning at its loom, sewing
Its webs of death and dinner, bat-squeaks
In moon-shadow, their flittermouse farewells.
Now, though, I'll go and whisper lullabies
To the traceless powdered butterflies
And all the little creatures that die in secret
Beyond imagination, mind, and wit.'

Older Poet to Younger Poets

Forbid morbidity. Time passes.
There's no necessity for sorrow,
Unless...Be active. Banish *alases*.
Force no more sighs; and ponder the sparrow.

Don't go out of your way to be improper—
You already are. Grow herbs on windowsills
(If you have them). There's no eavesdropper
On one who works alone, counting syllables,

Saying your lines aloud. Please, not on a train,
Or on a bus, or strolling down the street,
And never, never, *never* on a plane.
And 'twixt, and 'tween, and o'er, *are* obsolete.

So, cherish solitude for the sake of your songs.
Only your Muse, whoever She or He may be,
Your secret listener, pointing out your wrongs,
Your rights, can criticize your poetry.

Think in pictures. Think in rhythm. Then let
Others see and hear them too. Don't forget
Poetry can oblige you to be insolent—
Be so, if that is what you want.

Better still, attend to all five senses.
Make readers see, hear, taste, touch, and smell
Until your poem's narrative convinces
By what's disclosed, and casts its spell.

Live for that secular epiphany
That happens anywhere, that is lying to hand;
But beware the fraudulent and phoney
In anything you cannot understand.

Two years in a garret did no one harm
(And maybe not much good) but you'll get nowhere
Unless you take a risk and chance your arm.
Avoid too much indoors, though. Take the air.

Now, disregard everything I've written.
Turn everything I've said into what you say—
I know you're well and truly smitten.
You'll stay the course, but there's a price to pay.

And, for God's sake, learn how to cook.
No more pot noodles on the hoof!
Until you're famous, keep off the hard stuff.
If you've a mind to, send me your first book.

The Nothing-But

'He was beginning to live in the region of truth.'
Graham Greene, The Honorary Consul

Slowly the truth dawns, the nothing-butness of it,
The fly in the dram, the flea in your ear,
Just-cleaned window now smeared with dove-shit,
Confidence that turns into abject fear,
The niggle, the virtuous irritant,
A taste like garlic, chilli, or mint.

To have kissed the lips of one who was dying
Is to have tasted silence, salt, and wilderness,
And touched the truth, the desert where there is no lying,
Only that kiss and the keeping of its promise.
Who lives there, in that land of the utter truth?
Is it one of the delusions of youth,

Or the delusions of age and adulthood?
Well, I don't know. Only the truth will do,
I suppose, not would, or should, or could,
But what was, and is. Is it the same for you?
As the witty French say, 'reconstruct your virginity',
In search of beginnings and tranquillity.

Progress

There they are, widows of the professoriate
Tied to their frail routines, but not unfree
Wheeling their shopping zimmers on Market Street;
And octogenarian still-cycling emeriti
Cautious of cobbles and slow-moving cars
Hunting for elusive parking spaces—
Physicists, medics, classicists, astronomers.
Gladly I yield to their seniority,
Their ancient tweeds, their wrinkled faces.
I would like to be a venerable sage,
And might be yet, if I can reach that age,
Nodding off over a Loeb in the Library
Half-way through a forgotten declension,
Defeated, yet again, by Livy's prose.
But I gave up my bike ten years ago,
Terrified of traffic on the A91—
And that was on the pavement. I suppose
That so-called 'progress' overtakes us all—
Superfast fibre, electronic bravado.
Where will it end? That's what I want to know.
It's years since I last saw an icicle.

Curmudgeon

He is a man for whom everyone's a trespasser.
Co-existence? He doesn't believe in it.
Give you the time of day? Not one minute.
He is happy to be a grinning contrarian.
Music, he claims, gives him indigestion.
He dismisses several generations
Including most members of his own.
He is a virtuoso concert pessimist
Who even disagrees with his own agreements.
He is the exact opposite of mellow.
You never see him sitting in the sun.
And as for 'foreigners'—oh-ho!—
He is the Keeper of terms like 'wog' and 'dago'.
Longevity has failed to teach him benevolence.
I notice his visible weak spot
Spilling from the back of his eternal cap—
And I think he deserves my parting shot:
And so I say to him, 'Get your hair cut.'

Recipes and Refugees

I knew a student had a slogan in her car
And BORN TO SHOP, it said. Yes, BORN TO SHOP.
I'm in Tesco's. I wonder where you are.
In Harvey Nick's, or going over the top
In Jenner's with a plastic card? Poets' Day—
Piss Off Early, Tomorrow's Saturday.

I like Friday. I like the supermarket's
Bewildering choice, so much to eat and drink,
Or clean with. Or, or, or... The deficit's
Enormous in a glimpse, a single blink
That sums up plenitude and liberty,
Tyrannical famine, fear, and poverty.

How can a man be good, and kind, and true,
While knowing he's got more than many have
In hot, dry countries? What can I do?
Or you? Or you? It isn't very brave
To keep on shopping, though to stay alive
Means buying drink and dinner. I'll survive

Even worse torments of guilt and conscience.
Everyone else does. So, then, why can't I?
It feels worse being older, ever since
Remembering when there wasn't much to buy
Or cash to pay for the necessities.
Though not forgotten, these are far off days.

Affluence in exotic recipes—
The choice of what to cook is international.
I welcome that, but think of refugees
Drawing their water from a fly-blown well
In the land of falafels and couscous
Where sympathy is worse than useless.

I hope you've lost your shopper's selfish boast.
In our domestic daily lives, we choose,
We purchase, and we try to make the most,
Morally, of fish, salad, basmati, booze,
Pasta, olive oil, the occasional chop.
It's not just you. Everyone's BORN TO SHOP.

In a Volume of Dowson's

'To Florence, to combat the inexorable ennui'.
A perfect inscription, the fin de siècle
In anonymous ink, done to a T.
Or that's what it does for me.
I bought it back in the Age of the Turtleneck
And Baggy Corduroys, that era
Of Beatnik beards and my own Cynara,
That is, in Glasgow, 1963,
From a book-barrow in a lane off Renfield Street
Where all the good folk, book folk, jazz folk, used to meet.

I give in willingly to Decadent verse.
No tears are left to shed. My love is in it.
I cherish Dowson's phrases, his metres.
Reading Pierrot of the Minute,
The way we used to do (pictures by Beardsley)
Naked and pillowed on a quilted bed
In comfy Giffnock. Heavens, look at me
Reading our Dowson! She's gone and dead
Thirty-four years, and still I can't forget
Pillows and pages, kisses, love's palaver, and yet—

'Oh days of wine and roses'!
Simple love, straightforward love, and true love,
Love, oh careless love!…All life supposes
That that's the state that we're all dreaming of.
Yes, Yes, and Yes again. What else is there
Comforts or satisfies so much as nakedness
Under a downie and two hearts bare
In an inexpert youthful frantic kiss?
I think it's possible to love too much.
Days. Roses. Lilies. Kisses, wine, and touch.

What's decadence if not excessive love's
Too much of a good thing? Pre-Raphaelite
By disinclination, an Oscarian glove
As yellow as Browning's, a fondness for night,
A Francophil, a late Scoto-Parisian,
I might be out-of-time, a semi-pissed
Dowsonian, or Stevensonian,
A lavender proto-pre-Modernist—
At least, on nights like this that's how I feel,
Up late again, part Red, part black, part *eau de nil.*

The Glove Compartment

After her stroke, hers was the first to go.
It sat for two years in their garage, though,
All through the months of her recovery,
Though that was far from full. Vocabulary
Re-emerged, but slowly. So he retired
A few years earlier than anticipated.
He couldn't leave it all to the nurse he'd hired;
She said he shouldn't, but that's what he did.
'Please, sell my car. I'll never drive again.'
It seemed as final as a sung Amen.
He knew it must happen, but didn't know when.

When he opened her glove compartment
He found small change, lip salve, tissues, receipts
From shops and filling stations, peppermint,
An ice-scraper, lipstick, and boiled sweets,
Two tickets for a play at Dundee Rep
(Unused), all sorts of trivial stuff.
He shoved them in bag. Sat back and wept.
There's love in the world. But never enough.

Remembering Friends Who Feared Old Age
and Dementia More than Death

Even when just the other day
From Then to Now feels decades away.
The name at the back of the mind…
What can I say?
That memory's fickle, that fretting
Over a lost name or forgotten month
Makes you feel guilty, mindless, and blind,
That it's perfectly natural to fear the labyrinth
Where the 'ageing process' might one day take you
Into the land of forgetting?
You said it, friends. Too true.

Dictionaries become indispensable?
There's an urge to re-read the Bible?
That song was in *what* key?
Over the hill,
Round the corners, round the bends,
And *nuts* to you, too, as I check my diary
For wherever it is I'm supposed to be,
Today, or the next, that old clock-sorcery
I don't depend on, though I know I should,
And which you overdid, old friends.
No, I don't think you did,

Not now I'm older. No one
Looks forward to being old and alone,
The carer with a spoon,
Visitor gone,
Boredom and fright on television.
How do you understand the merry young
As you endure a dragging afternoon
With a hundred names on the tip of your tongue,
Unable to cheer yourself up,
In a constant state of indecision?
Cheers! Let's pour another cup.

Vicki Feaver: Riding a Wave

'Do it now, say it now, don't be afraid.'
Wilhelmina Barnes-Graham (1912–2004)

There's a photograph on my fridge of me in a wetsuit on a beach holding a surf-board. It was taken a couple of years ago on a holiday with my children and grandchildren. I put it there to remind me that I'm not too old to catch the momentum of a wave and enjoy the thrill of it carrying me to the shore. I can't stand up on the board like a real surfer. I ride it on my belly. Even so, it depends on catching the wave at precisely the right moment.

This is exactly what happened to me with the Baring Foundation's commission to write poems about ageing. I almost turned it down, fearful that I wouldn't be able write enough, or even any poems on the subject. But last year I'd tutored a workshop in the home of the Scottish painter Wilhelmina Barnes-Graham. Returning home, I pinned above my desk her dictum, written in her nineties, 'Do it now, say it now, don't be afraid.' Inspired by those words and the verve and ambition of the prints and paintings she worked on in her final years, I said, 'Yes'. The timing was perfect. I felt as if I was 'riding a wave'.

My initial idea was to write poems about artists who went on working into old age. In fact those poems, including 'The Blue Wave', about a painting by Wilhelmina Barnes-Graham, were written last. The first poems that emerged from jottings in my notebook are descriptions and meditations on my experience of ageing. I wrote about the fear of losing my memory. The 'old woman, pale and worried as a ghost', in 'Forgetfulness'—inspired by Keats' personification of Autumn in his Ode—is a terrifying vision of what I might become. I wrote about my fear of death 'following behind me in velvet slippers' in 'Death and the Maiden'. I wrote about how this fear sharpens the senses and increases the desire to live in the present. In 'Old Woman in a Forsythia Bush' I wrote about my vague belief in a creative energy, personified as 'a great puppeteer' who dangles lambs from strings:

and, now I'm old, whose arms
have dragged me through the long
dark corridors of another winter
to sit on this sunny seat, among
starry stems of forsythia,
buoyant again, as if sprung
from my body and floating
above it, like a seed flung
from the grey head of a dandelion.

The buoyancy, the sense of coming alive, arose directly from the
excitement of writing for the ageing project. The poems were written
in solitude. But meeting with Douglas Dunn and Diana Hendry and
sharing poems and ideas gave me the encouragement I thrive on.

*

Vicki Feaver was born in Nottingham in 1943. She retired as
Professor of Creative Writing at Chichester University in 2000
and moved with her husband to Dunsyre, in South Lanarkshire.
She has published three collections of poetry. The Handless
Maiden (1994) was awarded a Heinemann Prize and shortlisted
for the Forward Prize. The Book of Blood (2006) was shortlisted
for both the Costa and Forward Prizes. Her poem 'Judith' won
the Forward Prize for Best Single Poem. She has also received a
Cholmondeley Award and a Hawthornden Fellowship.

Forgetfulness

When my memory
was a film library
with a keen curator

who knew precisely
where to find clips
of every word

I wished unsaid,
or deed undone,
to play back to me

on sleepless nights,
I'd have welcomed her
muddling the reels.

But now the curator's
retired, the ordered
shelves are in chaos.

I roam the racks
without a guide
searching for scenes

I've lost. Sometimes,
unable to remember
what I'm searching for,

I find Forgetfulness
kneeling on the floor—
an old woman, pale

and worried as a ghost,
rummaging in a tangle
of shiny black ribbons.

The Larder

Turned seventy, and not wanting
to waste the days left, half-asleep,
I'm stocking the shelves of a larder.

Each day is an empty jar to fill:
yesterday, with the silvery teeth
on a leaf-lichen; the day before,

with a thin mist rolling slowly
across the valley, fading a line
of beeches to pencilled ghosts.

Today it's the powdery bloom
on the skin of a blueberry;
turning it, cold from the fridge,

between my thumb and finger;
noting the petal-shaped crater
where the flower shrivelled,

a small hole where it was pulled
from the stalk, crushing
its tangy pulp on my tongue.

Bone-House

bānhūs, bone-house: Old-English kenning for the body

It's not all fear and ruin.
I've always loved old houses
for the histories they hold,
their patina of use.

Old bodies are the same.
My hunched shoulders
and stiff neck, tell of hours
spent battling with words.

My belly-skin, stretched
by four babies, resembles
the rippled sand left behind
when the tide retreats.

My missing teeth reveal
a childhood of sugary treats,
my face's fretted lines,
a life-time as a worrier.

Foolish, when I think
how safe my life has been,
compared to warrior-poets
who twinned 'bone' with 'house'

to forge a stronger word
than 'body' as fortress
for flesh so vulnerable
to thrusts of spear and sword;

a better word—once
its spirit-guest had flown—
for the derelict frame,
picked clean by circling crows.

Pomegranate Juice

Head propped on pillows,
face spectral with the pallor
winter lends old skin,
I look out over the shining ridges
of my duvet's ice-field
and think of the poem

the Emperor Hadrian
addressed to his departing soul—
once joking companion,
already sombre and pale,
about to leave for colder
and colder regions.

Wondering what might revive
my soul—after months
without sun, resembling
a light-deprived, frost-
scorched pea-shoot—
I remember the beaker

of pomegranate juice
I bought from a stall
at the foot of the Citadel
in Erbil—freshly squeezed
from a revolving drum
of blood-red seeds—

the gleaming juice
Pluto shares with Persephone
to celebrate her autumnal
return to the Underworld.
The juice given to welcome
every new arrival.

Old Woman in a Forsythia Bush

Bright bush of yellow stars
reaching out to me with long
bowed wands, among fields,
ringing with blackbird songs;
where lambs, licked into life
by sheep's rough tongues,
leap like ballet dancers,
impossibly high, as if hung
on strings of a great puppeteer
who dangled me when young,
exciting me to strip off vest
and bra to celebrate spring;
and, now I'm old, whose arms
have dragged me through the long
dark corridors of another winter
to sit on this sunny seat, among
starry stems of forsythia,
buoyant again, as if sprung
from my body and floating
above it, like a seed flung
from the grey head of dandelion.

The Mower

When I was young and miserable,
a misfit and a rebel,
almost never out of trouble,
desperate to escape school,
time dawdled.
                    But now I'm older
and happier and want it to go slower,
time's an out-of-control mower
careering through the borders
decapitating all the flowers.

Travelling

My sister and I drank Buck's Fizz
on Christmas Day, on the deck
of a cruise ship in the Indian Ocean,

with three women in their late eighties
(two minus breasts, one with a metal hip)—
all, like Tennyson's restless elderly Ulysses,

buoyed by the belief that by living
permanently at sea they could go on
circling the globe's oceans, and sitting

at the captain's table, for ever.
No one mentioned the passenger,
slipped discreetly ashore in a coffin.

But even sitting here, in the lamplight
of early evening at home, hand tacking
across a notebook's blank pages,

I'm travelling: forwards at time's pace,
and backwards and forwards
at the mind's speeds, as is Floss,

my deaf, almost blind old dog,
who's lying beside me,
quivering and yelping in a dream

of running through rushes,
and startling a partridge
to lift into the sky like a rocket.

The Blue Wave

'Do it now, say it now, don't be afraid.'
Wilhelmina Barnes-Graham

Your house with its lovely
light studio overlooking the sea
is sold, your work dispersed.

But in my head there's a painting
done in your nineties
when just to lift your arm

was an effort: a single brave
upwards sweep with a wide
distemper brush so loaded

with paint the canvas filled
with the glistening blue wall
of a wave before it falls.

The Old Fir-Tree

after a painting by Emily Carr

Younger, you'd scramble
over fallen trunks and branches,
escaped from home
to sketch deep in the forest.
Lighting a cigarette,

blowing smoke rings
to banish clouds of midges,
you'd wait, breathing tobacco
mingled with needle-mulch
and pine resin, tuning in

to the voices and rhythms
of the trees, before, charcoal
in hand, following the dance
of the branches, whirling up
to reach sunlight.

Frailer as you aged, you sat
on a stool at the forest's edge,
a large sheet of brown paper
pinned to a board on your knee,
with brushes, oil paints,

and cheap gasoline
for thinning, at your feet.
Gazing up at this ancient fir—
as you had at the totem poles
of the Haida, and the black

implacable pillar of your grief-
angry widowed father—
you painted the spikes
of broken-off branches
outlined against pale sky,

the dark bark of a trunk,
so tall you had to lop the top
to fit the paper, and so wide
you couldn't reach your arms
round it, if you tried.

Swimming In Old Age

Descending the steps
of a small deserted pool
in a Cretan hotel, I'm as excited
as if I've slipped like a snake
out of old skin and am again
a girl on a Pembrokeshire beach—
intoxicated by reading Lawrence's
Women in Love, and the scent
of violets and pink thrift
on the cliffs—stripping off
and swimming naked.

Plunging into briny sea,
or the weed-smelling water
of lakes and river pools,
I returned to the element
where, if I hadn't lost
fish's gills as a foetus,
I was meant to live.

Wading over blue tiles
on the pool floor—water
creeping up the skin
of my thighs, belly and breasts,
until, almost out of my depth,
I reach out with my arms,
push off with my feet,
and, neck too stiff to lift
my head above water,
flounder, panicking
like a child who can't swim.

Dreams of Flying

As a child, blowing out
birthday candles in one puff,
I'd make a wish to be able to fly.

I wanted to live at the top of a tower,
in a room with a trapdoor in the floor
to keep out people I didn't like.

I've ended up in a bungalow,
in a valley hemmed in by hills,
often cut off by snow, but under

the flight-path of wintering
pink-foot geese, honking overhead
in a language as unintelligible

as the wavering script they scrawl
across the sky. When they leave—
heading for Greenland in spring—

I watch buzzards riding thermals,
or attacked by angry crows, flocks
of gulls driven inland by gales.

On still days, hot-air balloons,
striped turquoise and lemon,
rise from a gap between pines.

I'd be afraid to go up in a basket.
I get out of breath climbing stairs.
But in my sleep I soar—lifting off

without wings, or even flapping
my arms. If only I had faith
I could do it awake: trapped

by snow, or infirmity,
or vexing visitors, escaping—
whoosh—through an open window.

Clementines

Past their best—
when the thin peel
could be stripped off

exposing naked
orange fruits, bursting
with sweet juice—

they're dried up,
shrinking, ready
for the waste bin.

But I'm of an age
to want to honour
their ageing:

faint grooves
between the segments
deepening;

glowing colour
dulling and
darkening;

to bear witness
as they collapse in
on themselves—

spent suns, casting
umber shadows
in the white dish.

Second Childhood

Last scene of all,
That ends this strange eventful history,
Is second childishness...

As You Like It, II. *vii*

Some return, having lost
every memory in between,
to the only place they feel at home.

Others, like the survivors
of a war, are compelled
to relive its traumas.

Even those who bolt
the door on childhood
return involuntarily in sleep.

I dreamed of my ashes,
swilling with plankton
in the ocean's currents,

washed up on a beach
where a child in a sunsuit
sits like a faithful guard dog

beside her grandmother—
who's dozing in a deckchair,
wearing a black straw hat,

thick lisle stockings
and lace-up shoes—
a child with two plaits

and a pale, pinched face,
digging her bare toes
into grains of sand.

Costume Boxes

The first, a dressing-up drawer,
was stuffed with my mother's
discarded dresses, skirts so long
that even hitched up at the waist,
I tripped over the hems.

The second, a wicker trunk,
was filled with costumes
for school plays: ruffs, crowns,
codpieces, and the beaded gown
I wore as Beatrice in Much Ado.

The third, a shoe box, a mouse
has invaded, tearing at card
and tissue, gnawing holes
in hand-knit bootees, a pale
turquoise wool baby dress.

The last, an iron chest, holds
clothes you can't choose or swap:
the shrinking skins of cancers,
grey gauze veils of grief, coats
with pockets full of stones.

Prayer at Seventy

God of thresholds, guide
of souls between worlds,
have mercy on me

who when I asked you
if I could pass my last years
with less anxiety

changed me into a tiny spider
launching into the unknown
on a thread of gossamer

and when I begged you
to let me be a bigger
fiercer creature

into a polar bear
leaping between
melting ice floes.

Death and the Maiden

He was there at my birth:
watching as I was delivered,
doll-size, six weeks early,
to a mother with blood-
pressure perilously high.

He stayed for my first cry:
then left, no longer interested
until my appendix threatened
to burst on a caravan holiday
in Wales. I was eleven:

next to me on the ward,
a woman who confided
'Half my stomach's missing!'
and passed me a copy
of *True Life Romances*.

One night, the curtains closed
round her bed. Next morning,
it was empty. He'd gone too,
refusing to return, even when
I called him, crying bitterly.

Though, when I swallowed
a whole bottle of pills,
he arrived to whisper,
'Silly girl!' And he raced
to the lonely lake where a man

took off his tie to strangle me
and when I opened my mouth
to scream, no sound came out.

He pinned him to the ground,
while I ran into the trees.

He saved me again
when I swam too far out
into cold Cornish sea
and, too tired to struggle
against the current,

let my mouth and nose
slip under the water.
He cupped my chin in his hand,
holding it above the waves
until I reached the beach.

And when I rode pillion
on a motorbike, doing a ton
on the switchback road
that runs along the Roman Wall
in Northumberland,

not caring if I held on
or let go, I felt his arms
holding tight round my waist.
After that I didn't think
of him for years.

And he'd no reason
to think of me. But now,
though I can't see or hear him,
I sense he's back: following
behind me in velvet slippers.

Instructions for My Funeral

When I read about the body
of the drowned Shelley
being burned on a beach,
I thought 'that's what I want!'
Then I remembered the smell

of bones boiled dry in a pan
left to burn on the stove,
so I'll settle for a regular
cremation and beach picnic
with a driftwood bonfire.

Food should suit the season
and weather. But sun or rain,
the wine must be amarone
that makes me think of Keats'
'vintage cool'd a long age

in the deep delved earth',
and the poem he wrote,
hearing the plaintive song
of a nightingale, to ease
the grief of his brother dying.

Then, music and dancing:
old and young partnered
together, as in Paula Rego's
painting of a family circling
on a moonlit cliff-top.

Dancing's the only thing
I feel I've missed out on.
If I'm there, I want Death
to let me stand on his toes
and waltz me over the sea.

Diana Hendry: Off / On Joy

> How nerve-wracking it is to be getting old, how much better to be old!
> Muriel Spark, *Memento Mori*

Of the many definitions of a poem, I've long treasured one by Helen Vendler— 'a poem is a voice participating in a very long and very old conversation about life.' As both reader and writer, it's the *participating in a conversation* that appeals. Perhaps the most enjoyable and valuable part of this Baring Foundation commission has been sharing it with two other poets, Douglas Dunn and Vicki Feaver. In meeting, talking about and workshopping poems, we have been participating in that conversation. I hope the poems here continue it.

Creative Ageing—our topic. I've come to dislike the word 'creative' which seems to imply some kind of virtue. Creative or not, it's hard to keep focused on ageing. The mind keeps shifting away from it, not least because inevitably it leads to thoughts of death, but also because although we are creatures bound by time, in some ways we are not of time. Our consciousness is other. Consciousness shifts about in centuries, can leap us back to childhood. In our heads and hearts and minds we are astonishingly free.

But death is something I've thought about since I was eight, which was when my grandma died—mysteriously disappearing so that I thought she had folded herself up like a flower does at night and slid herself into one of the two urns she kept on her windowsill.

At the start of this commission I found myself nervously returning to the books I read in my troubled thirties—Jung, Simone Weil, Maritain; books with terrible titles like Kierkegaard's *Fear and Trembling and the Sickness Unto Death*. What was I after? Belated wisdom? Such books no longer spoke to my condition. I was more at home with the joyous American poet Alicia Suskin Ostriker and her lines:

I want to live
said the old woman
like a flame in flight *

Working on these poems I've counted up my losses of friends and family
(mostly recently a sister) and pondered other losses, of looks, physical
strength, expectations. But as hunger sharpens the appetite, so age
intensifies one's awareness of the beauty and wonder of the world,
of love and of blessings. Mixed in with grief and sorrow is a kind of
off / on joy.

Recently, while on holiday in Orkney I came across The Which? Guide
to Active Retirement (1993). I found it rather more depressing than
Kierkegaard for its focus was almost entirely on looking after oneself.
It was practical and responsible, advocating a sensible if dull content-
ment. The Guide made me remember my youthful desire to end my life
spent—that is to use whatever I possessed in the way of energy, passion,
ability—to the hilt. That's still how I'd like to end.

* The Old Woman, the Tulip and the Dog by Alice Suskin Ostriker
(University of Pittsburgh Press, 2014).

*

Diana Hendry (born 1941) lives in Edinburgh. She has published
six collections of poetry, most recently The Seed-box Lantern: New
& Selected Poems (2013). She has published more than forty books
for children, including Harvey Angell which won a Whitbread
Award in 1991, and The Seeing (2012), which was shortlisted both
for a Costa Award and a Scottish Children's Book Award.

Callers

Perhaps being old is having lighted rooms
Inside your head ....
                        Philip Larkin

Well yes, maybe I am an old fool
For there is a lighted room inside my head
Where folk I know—alive and dead—come to call.
It's like the foyer of a grand hotel,
And though I'm out of sight I watch them all.

Often it's my children, as they were when small.
Yesterday a friend I haven't seen for years,
My brother-in-law who died last spring,
And a girl I used to know quite well at school.

None of them stays long or knows they're here.
I watch them look about then hurry on.
It pleases me to think I might appear
As guest or ghost in lighted rooms elsewhere.

The House Where I Was Born

The ghosts are easy. I can switch them on
like a tv soap. Here's Pa going up the stairs,
flip flap, the flattened back of his slippers
and Ma in the kitchen, her cigarette ash stretching
precariously over the black frying pan. One sister
in her room of make-up, petticoats, sequins;
the other sobbing over her boarding school trunk
and my various selves flitting about, age this
that, the other. Here I am—flash—and here—
and here. Do I really have to say The Lord's Prayer
twenty times without making a mistake? Am I
still at it? Voices in the garden. The cough
on the stairs. The wooden gate. Spots of time.
The house that mothered me more than mother.

Somehow the memory of it's gone shabby
as if it needs fresh paint, the windows cleaned.
A silent, sullen child stares out, closes the door.

Autobiography

And what d'you remember of sorrow, child?

I remember when she went away
the house turned chill, my breastbone ached.

And what d'you remember of fear, child?

Long grass, bare feet, imagined snakes.
Dark slid a lid across the day.

And what d'you remember of jealousy, child?

I remember the sister my school friend had—
her chuckly gran and her airman dad.

And what d'you remember of love, child?

I remember the sailor who took my heart—
the salt of his skin, the nights apart.

And what d'you remember of happiness, child?

The song of the sea and its constancy
and all the passions it promised me.

Beyond

Nothing so lovely as   the hoot
                  of a distant train
running through your dream.

                  Is it childhood
you're listening to, worlds going off the map,
or infinity?

Always you liked views that spoke of beyond—
those seascapes stretching out that didn't stop at sky but went on…

What is it about the need for it? The why
of flight   mountaineering   the gift of grace.   How dire

if ours was the only galaxy!

How happily the word sits in the mouth, satisfying
as a communion wafer.

This is the sound of the distant train
                  running through your dream—

be-yond be-yond be-yond be-yond

Parting

i.m. Julie Betty Rowan

Early autumn the school trunk would re-appear
as if to say summer was over, time for my sister to disappear.

She was the homely one my mother loved too much.
A North Wales boarding school, my father's mute reproach.

Me—an avid reader of all Blyton's stories of St Clare's—
they kept at home, unaware I longed to go and envied her.

The trunk seemed huge, as deep as sorrow and in it
every vest and sock was named—only love went missing.

I remember most the heavy winter coat she had to wear—
grey as the railway station full of girls, grief in the parting air.

*

And now she's gone, the sister I didn't see
for more than twenty years. O there were letters

now and then and phone calls, but mostly
between us nothing but distance and neglect.

So now I find a deadness in my heart
and numbness where the pain should be.

To friends I say 'we grew apart,
had nothing in common', though what can compare

with those early years of childhood shared?

Teeth

My mother must have been in her forties
when first her bottom, then her top teeth
were removed. I remember her huddled
over the electric fire, spitting blood
into a small white pudding basin.
It was the day she lost her youth.

Dentistry's come a long way since then,
so though literally I'm a little long
in the tooth, mine are hanging in there,
flossed and polished, sans bridge or
crown. My unwhitened smile suggests
a dirty grin. Some days I think

all life is a process of weaning. First
the breast, then fags, now the dentist
shaking his head at my mint imperials.

The Cut

It takes years off you, he said, at which point
I reached into my snake print tote bag
and took out my Smith & Wesson 642
Syn Grips, 5 shot. Stand by your driers,
I said, throw down your scissors. They had
Long Brown Wavy Hair on the loop—
I cut it short. OK, I said, hand 'em over,
you got my years. Goddamit, they were all
over the parquet! So much silver you could
have stuffed a cushion. Each year
something special, unrepeatable, unique.
I left them crawling about the floor,
blondie still weeping.

Charades with Freya (7)

Animals are easy. I can do penguin waddle,
hoppy frog, snappy croc. And Actions—all
those ings—dancing, eating, sleeping—are a doddle.

It's Objects that test me to my limits. To become guitar
I must hollow out the sound-hole of my heart;
open the door of myself to become room;
let go of love to lift the lighthearted balloon.
How get the measure of myself and become ruler?
Where's the river god to turn me into tree? How flower?

Animals, Actions, Objects—we put the cards back in the tin.
Quick as a flash I'm gran.

Meditation on an Old Bear

He's what happens when you're very old
And you've lost your fur and you're ever so cold
And your smile's stitched on and you're coming undone
And whatever stiffened your spine has gone
And your paws are worn and your skin so thin
That anyone looking can see right in
And your ears are frayed and your nose is squashed
And your chest is darned and your eyes are crossed
And you sit on a shelf propped up by a wall
And nothing can stop your decline and fall.

The Widow

No bread or sugar in the house
as if life's staff and sweetness left
with him. No-one's told his chair
he won't be back or changed the light
that falls, as always, on the sofa's
faded patch. The kitchen plates
can't find their shelves, the furniture's
in shock, and everywhere's disturbance
like a night raid's aftermath,
the scene left by an intruder
when the loot of love's been snatched.

Within my awkward hug she's brittle
as a twig that pity's touch might snap.

Insomnia

Some nights it waits for me,
sneaks into my head as soon as I lie down,
opens everything up, raising the shutters,
flinging open doors and and windows
as if there's a shopping mall in my brain
and some poor crazed soul's sent in
to visit all the little booths of thought,
the drug stores of philosophy,
the boutiques of regrets, the muddled rags
of memories going cheap on market stalls.

And there's no rest, no pause to settle,
consider, compose a decent sentence.
Insomnia has the poor crazed soul
in thrall, drives it on to flit
from half thought to half thought,
memory scrap to lost thread,
notes, nudges, something just out of reach.

And then the body joins in—a crick
in the neck. Restless legs, burning feet,
an ache in the back, in the heart
in the dark, dark, dark.
It's six a.m. when insomnia slopes off.

An Alternative Retirement

Something in the heart rejoices at a certain kind of wickedness—
the audacious crime in which no-one gets hurt, the derring-do,
the risk, the danger, the glamorous gang riding off with the loot.

So this was the Hatton Garden Heist. Eight of them
on Good Friday night, the city quiet, the police asleep,
sliding down the disabled lift shaft, boring a hole
through a concrete wall, rifling through the boxes in the vault,
escaping, after two nights work, with a haul

of diamonds to outshine the stars. And oh, it stirs
the stumps to learn that two of the gang are seventy plus!
Time to re-think retirement. Forget the garden, macrame,
looking after the grandchildren. Think of the fun
to be had on the long winter nights, planning a heist.

For surely we all, in one way or another, want to say
I got away with it? So here's to the Hatton Garden Eight
who almost did and to those others in the lists
of loveable villains—Robin Hood, the Artful Dodger, my grandad.

My First Love

I made the mistake of getting in touch with him
twenty years after—invited him to stay.
He was almost alcoholic, had lost his front teeth,
told endless anecdotes and, worst of all,
was allergic to my dog. You'd think that'd be
a cure or antidote to all those years of unrequited love
spent yearning and longing, that I could forget
that time—was I seventeen?—when he asked me
to go with him to the States, could forget that moment
years later when, at long long last he proposed,
could forget that because I was young and fearful
and he was wild, arty and penniless, I kept saying no.
Less easy to forget how, ever since, I've wondered...

Watching Telly With You

We could go to Paris of course
but not so often. And it might not be quite
as cosy as the sofa, the fire, our slippers,
the zapper. Sometimes mid-morning
I think about it, hankering a little like
the lovelorn do, for that evening lull,
front door locked, feet up, snugged up,
loved up and watching telly with you.

Timor mortis conturbat me*

Will it give me six months warning
Or come when least expected?
Will I trip over it one morning
And find myself disconnected?

Will it come on the way to Corstorphine
Or when sitting on the loo?
Will I need a lot of morphine
Will a bottle of brandy do?

Will it happen in broad daylight
Or wait until it's dark?
Will it come like a lover at midnight
On a necromancing lark?

Will I lose control of my bladder?
Will I lose control of myself?
Will the Lord send down a ladder
And shock the National Health?

Will it start as a minor chill,
Then turn to a nasty cough?
Will it spread everywhere until
Someone has to switch me off?

Is it already growing inside me?
Does it have a date and a time?
Will I know when at last it's untied me?
O what's the use of rhyme?

*'The fear of death disturbs me', a phrase from the Catholic Office of the Dead, was used notably by William Dunbar, the medieval Scottish poet, in his 'Lament for the Makars'.

End Matter

i. You're at the postscript stage,* I read.
    What to say but sorry, thank you,
    blessings, praise?

ii. Have you done all you could?
    All that was in you to do?
    Please leave the house tidy.

iii. I used to ask, who was I
    to talk about the moon, war,
    the bickering of men in the city?
    But if not me, awkward, inept,
    mostly foolish, who?

iv. The furniture of the house needs renewing.
    The furniture of my heart and mind, ditto.

v. Forget purple.
    Think cashmere.

vi. What to do with the smallness of my life
    is such an enormous question.

*Dennis O'Driscoll

The Last Piano

If there were seven ages of piano
this would be the last—the sound
heard through the wall of my old neighbour
repeating her stumbling pieces like prayers.

Not music, more an SOS strummed
on the air, a call of distress from one
who plays to save herself drowning
in silence. It haunts the night,

the maroon that calls the lifeboat out.
Tonight it's *Sur la Glace à Sweet Briar*.
Ragged arpeggios stagger and fall.
The piano's long been out of tune

and swollen knuckles stiffen her fingers
but still she persists, making
the difficult changes from major
to minor, minding the sharps and flats,

until she's got it off pat and skaters
go gliding over the ivory ice of Sweet Briar
and on the silence she's cut a star.

Praise Poem

Sunday afternoon and we're off for a walk to the lake
to see the swans' new cygnets. It's May, leafy and lush
and I'm at an age when I hanker after all new-born creatures.
Besides, I've an itch to write a praise poem, so as we walk
down the Holly Path I'm rejoicing in the beautiful way
trees age and rejoicing too in Simone Weil's thought
that it's the light from heaven that gives a tree
the energy to send its roots deep into the earth so that
The tree is really rooted in the sky. Then we see

one cygnet. Its parents glide about it—sweet scrap
of grey fluff—describing a shape that makes it a home.
There's a small audience on the bank, children
with bread, dads with cameras—elsewhere families
sunbathing, picnicking, sailing model boats. From here
we can see the castle on the hill and the three spires
of St Mary's—it's an idyll: trees, shining water, new life,
grandly mythical swans, sunshine—all the ingredients
for a perfect praise poem. And then I turn my head

and see him, the heron, standing stock still in the watery
rushes, watching and waiting, blatant as death. The locals
say there were five eggs, now there's only one cygnet. I flap
my arms at him, shout to shoo him away. He neither blinks nor
looks at me, stays there, fixed in his shabby, ragged robes,
threatening both the cygnet and my praise poem until

I remember the width and grandeur of his wings when he flies
down river and know there can't be a praise poem without him.